DAN MARINO

MY LIFE IN FOOTBALL

FOREWORD BY DON SHULA

Photographs by Marc Serota
Text by Dan Marino
with Dave Hyde

TRIUMPH
BOOKS

CHICAGO

DEDICATION

I dedicate this pictorial autobiography to my family, friends, and the fans who have supported me
so much through what has now ultimately been deemed a Hall of Fame NFL career.

My mother and father created the foundation that has made all of this possible,
and I am forever indebted to them for their undying love and support. Without their guidance
I would not be able to enjoy the successes of raising a loving family nor would I have experienced
the rewards of playing in the National Football League. My mom and dad set the examples that
have made my sisters and me the people we are today, and for that I will remain eternally grateful.

Sharing my career and achievements on and off the football field with my wife, Claire,
and my children, Alexandra, Daniel, Michael, Joey, Niki, and Lia, provides me with a daily
reminder of the joy and happiness for which I am so thankful to have in my life.
And to all the players I've suited up with, from St. Regis grade school and Central Catholic High
School, to the University of Pittsburgh and the National Football League, you guys are also my
family, and I thank you all from the bottom of my heart!

13

CONTENTS

Foreword by Don Shula   6

Introduction   12

The Early Years   36

Family Life   56

A Hall of Fame Career   92

Living the Dream   150

Giving Back   170

Memories and Mementos   182

6

foreword

We can't get him . . . can we?

That's what I was thinking as the hours ticked by in our draft room that day, April 26, 1983. Teams kept picking. Names kept being called. Quarterbacks kept going off our draft board all afternoon, though in a somewhat surprising manner for us coaches and scouts watching at Dolphins headquarters. Entering that day, here's how we ranked the first-round quarterbacks:

1. John Elway

2. Dan Marino

3. Jim Kelly

I've never forgotten the order. Elway went first to the Colts, Kelly went 13th to Buffalo, and we didn't have another quarterback rated for the first round. Not Todd Blackledge, who went seventh to Kansas City. Not Tony Eason, who went 14th to New England. Not Ken O'Brien, who went to the New York Jets in the final, fortunate surprise for us.

I knew the Jets needed a quarterback, I just had no idea who O'Brien even was at the time.

So that's how we were lucky enough to draft Dan and how I came to coach him for 13 of his 17 seasons. He broke every passing record in that time. Touchdowns. Completions. Passing yards. Whenever someone asks me what it was like to coach him, I answer in one word.

Just one.

"Excitement," I say.

When we brought Dan to camp as a rookie, everyone saw his talent. The first passing drill we'd run each practice had receivers line up wide on both sides of the quarterback. David Woodley, our incumbent starter who relied more on athleticism than his arm, threw to a receiver running a pattern on one side. Then Dan stepped in and threw to a receiver on the other.

David threw . . . then Dan threw.

David threw . . . then Dan threw.

The difference was startling. That isn't meant as a criticism of David. I liked him a lot. He helped us win plenty. He was an NFL talent who quarterbacked the Dolphins to the Super Bowl the previous year. But practice sessions such as this underlined what a singular talent Dan was, right from the start.

The games quickly confirmed as much. Maybe the famous game against the 1985 Bears best explains Dan's ability. That Monday night stage was bigger than any regular-season game I played. The Bears were undefeated and so were we. They had that "46 Defense" with its blitz-and-destroy philosophy. Most teams kept extra blockers in to protect against that blitz. With our team, centered on Dan's arm and his uncanny ability to keep from being sacked, we did the opposite.

We spread them out with four receivers. We wanted our receivers to go one-on-one against their safeties. We came out and scored 31 points in the first half. It was the best half of offense I was ever associated with. We were so precise, in fact, that I later heard Bears coach Mike Ditka and defensive coordinator Buddy Ryan nearly came to blows at halftime while arguing how to defend us in the second half. Dan ended up throwing three touchdowns as we won, 38–24, and assured the undefeated 1972 Dolphin team I coached wouldn't have any company that year.

For each of Dan's 13 seasons with me, we had the same talk of establishing a running game to help him. We never found a top-tier running back, though we tried. We didn't have a dominant offensive line the way power running teams did, either. But

9

Shaking hands with coach Shula after throwing the record-breaking 343rd career touchdown pass in Indianapolis.

there I'd be every training camp, telling reporters, "We're going to establish the running game," and "This year we'll get the running game going."

But let's be serious: every defensive coach in the NFL would've liked us to establish a running game. Or try. It would have made their job easier. Understand, I'm not saying we weren't hoping to get some more balance between passing and running. But Dan's passing was the kind of strength you didn't strategically stray from. You couldn't. At least, not if you wanted to win.

I've been blessed with great quarterbacks in my coaching career. Each one was different. It started in Baltimore with John Unitas, who would hold the ball, and hold it, and just before getting hit, he'd throw it. He'd then peel himself off the ground and do it again. Bob Griese was a field general, smart and cool and so unselfish he'd utilize a great running game even if it meant he hardly threw the ball in an afternoon. Earl Morrall was resourceful enough to step in for Unitas one year and become the NFL's Most Valuable Player, and then step in for Griese another year and keep us going to the Perfect Season.

Dan was the best passer in NFL history. Didn't he pass for more touchdowns and yards than anyone else? Didn't he have 25 NFL passing records when he retired? Isn't that how you measure success?

As I write this in the spring of 2005, I'm making plans to attend Dan's Hall of Fame induction ceremony in August. I enjoyed the relationship with him as much or more than any I've had in my coaching career. Everyone knew he'd end up in Canton, too. I'm just glad, once again, he ends up there as a Dolphin.

We weren't just fortunate to get him that draft day.

We were fortunate to have him every day of his career.

—*Don Shula*

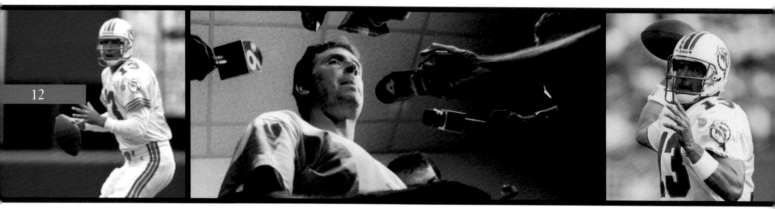

12

introduction

All right, I can confess now: I splurged upon arriving in Miami to start my NFL life. This was the summer of 1983, I had some money in my pocket for the first time, and I got every material thing I needed. Everything I dreamed of, really.

Bought a new stereo.

Rented a two-bedroom condo on Hollywood Beach. Got a new invention, the satellite TV dish, for my parents so they could watch Dolphins games back home in Pittsburgh (our backyard was so small and a dish so big back then that the buckeye tree shading the yard had to be cut down to accommodate it).

And, well, that was it. That was my entire, extravagant, hot-shot-rookie shopping spree. Seriously. I had received a Jeep Cherokee as MVP of the Senior Bowl, and when you add a place to sleep, some tunes, and a gift for Mom and Dad, what more could a 21-year-old bachelor need? Or want?

Besides a football to throw, that is.

That's the real point of starting my story here. You can see what mattered to me, right from my start with the Dolphins. Football is what I loved. Football is what drove me. Football always has been my singular passion and constant companion. I've been fortunate enough to travel the world, appear in movies, be in music videos, grace the most popular magazine covers, talk on the biggest TV shows, and get to know some of the world's most famous celebrities. All that is nice. It's wonderful, really. But nothing gave me a rush quite like running out with the team for a big game, in a packed stadium, on a Sunday on a sunny afternoon. Or Saturday on a snowy evening. Or Monday on a nationally televised night. It didn't matter when or where. Throwing a football brought me the most fun and the biggest

13

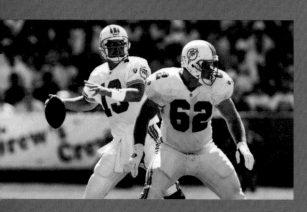

pleasure of anything outside of my family.

There's no feeling quite like seeing a receiver and a defend-er running downfield with so little space between them that it wouldn't fit under a door—and still thinking you can put a pass right in there. *Knowing it*, actually. And then throwing the football like a fastball so the defender can only shake his head as it zips by. His knowing only adds to the feeling: he had great coverage and he couldn't do anything! Mark Duper used to say how he'd run 40 yards downfield with a cornerback on him like a hip pad, make a little move, turn for the ball, and—whap!—the ball actually would stick in his hands before he even saw it.

Throwing a ball like that, my friends, is pure fun. It's magic. It's how I spent some of the best days of my life, game after game, year after year, until the seasons flew by, the touchdowns piled up, the record books went to rewrite, the legs ultimately wore out, and I was on my way to Canton.

Funny, isn't it, how such a public place like a football stadium could feel like my private playground? When I arrived in the league, writers wondered about the pres-sure of playing quarterback, before a full stadium, on national TV, with big stakes rid-ing on each play. That cracked me up. Pressure? That's where I belonged. It's what I loved to do. It's what I grew up dreaming about, too, from the moment my dad took me aside as a kid and said, "I think if you work hard, set your mind to it, and are lucky enough to stay healthy, you can become a pretty good athlete."

I was maybe 10 then. I was throwing at anything outside my home on Parkview

Avenue, in the Oakland section of Pittsburgh, just to feel myself gun the ball. Stop signs. Telephone poles. Neighbors. Anything at all. People ask all the time when I realized I had an industrial-strength right arm, but the truth is I don't ever remember otherwise. You know how you have brown hair or blue eyes? Well, that's kind of how I knew about my arm. It was just part of me.

I played pitcher and shortstop in baseball. I never played a position other than quarterback in football. Even in neighborhood pickup games, playing with kids three or four years older than I was, I'd be chosen to play quarterback. There was always some game going in our neighborhood, too. We'd play outside my home, stopping to let cars go by. We'd play at the St. Regis Elementary School playground a few houses down, where I attended school and played from fifth to eighth grade. We'd play in the field at the end of the street, too, which is where my dad and I would go by the hour to throw the football or field ground balls. We did it for fun, but he taught me, too: Here's how you hold the ball. Here's how you throw it. Here's how you practice.

A lot of lifelong habits were formed on that field in those days. Enough so that today it's called Dan

With Dad, Dan Sr., at the dedication of Dan Marino Field in Pittsburgh.

Marino Field. Enough, too, so that when I arrived at the University of Pittsburgh, coach Jackie Sherrill watched me throw as a freshman and pulled me over.

"Who taught you to throw?" he asked.

"My dad," I said.

"Listen to me," he said. "Whatever you do, don't let anybody tell you to do anything different. Just keep doing exactly what you're doing."

Later, Sherrill called it one of his best coaching tips ever.

The 50-yard line at Pitt was a 10-minute walk from the house I grew up in. It was also just down Fifth Avenue from Central Catholic High School, the city's football power, which I also attended. And that small triangle—St. Regis, Central Catholic, and Pitt—comprised my entire world until I came to the Dolphins. Three teams, 12 years, and all maybe 15 minutes apart. All with similar philosophies on football and life—sometimes with the philosophy being football was life.

I can still remember my fifth-grade team at St. Regis, kneeling in a church pew each Saturday morning, shoulder pad to shoulder pad.

"Our Father . . . ," the priest began.

"Who art in heaven . . . ," we all answered.

16

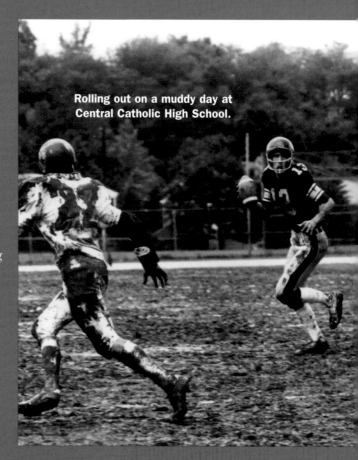

Rolling out on a muddy day at Central Catholic High School.

After praying we would stand up, and the cheerleaders would lead us out of the church, down the street, and through the neighborhood for our game. You might say God was on our side. Of course, this was a church league. He was on everyone's side.

But my childhood story was typical in that neighborhood. For instance, Wally Walczak, who was two years older and grew up right across from me on Parkview Avenue, preceded me at St. Regis and then as the starting quarterback at Central Catholic. And, just like I followed Wally up the line, he followed another kid from the neighborhood, David Degmer.

That gives you an idea of how sports-crazed this working-class and ethnic-heavy neighborhood was. My dad's side of the family came from Italy; my mom's side from Poland. And my dad had grown up there, right down the street from where I did. Some people say that none of us really leave our childhood neighborhood, no matter how far we move away and how many years have passed.

I know I haven't. If you want to understand who I am and what I became, just walk down the Parkview Avenue of my youth. It taught family values. It also taught toughness, competitiveness, sacrifice, and the importance of hard work.

It was there, in a youth baseball league, that I wore No. 13 for the first time. It wasn't exactly by design. Three of us were larger than the other kids. There were three big jerseys, Nos. 13, 14, and 15. And my dad was coach.

"It wouldn't look right if you picked your jersey before they did," he told me. Moved by superstition, they took Nos. 14 and 15.

I had No. 13 for life. That's just how things worked in our neighborhood. I even had a real job. I worked for Johnny Rosato's Lawn Service over a summer during high school. Cutting grass. Pulling weeds. Johnny once drove my crew to a hillside in the heat of a Pittsburgh summer and told us to mow it. Whew! We did the work. I also flipped a lawn mower that day and nearly cut off my toes. I promised myself then that I'd never have that kind of job for long, that sports was going to be my ticket.

The only question back then was whether I'd play baseball or football. I loved

them both. At Central Catholic, pro baseball scouts and college football recruiters came calling. I visited colleges that had strong programs in each sport:

Clemson, Florida State, Arizona State. The Kansas City Royals picked me in the fourth round of the same 1979 draft that they used an 18th-round choice on a guy whose path I'd crisscross in the coming years. Someone named John Elway. Those Royals scouts knew their stuff. I mean, how many teams pick two Hall of Famers in the same draft?

The problem was the Royals offered me $35,000 to sign. This was when the NCAA was just beginning to allow players to compete as amateurs in one sport and play professionally in another. You couldn't accept a scholarship, though. You had to pay tuition, so you had to earn enough money in the pros to offset that. Danny Ainge was the first to do it, and my dad called Ainge's father to find how it worked out. He also talked with the dad of Kirk Gibson, who played both sports at Michigan State.

Ultimately, Dad and I figured that between paying for tuition and living somewhere in the minor leagues it would end up costing me money to take the Royals' offer. And so, ultimately, I decided to ditch baseball altogether and stay home at Pitt. I could dump off laundry with Mom, have the occasional dinner at home, and still play in one of the nation's best programs.

Signing the letter of intent to play at Pitt, with Mom, Veronica, and Dad looking on.

My sophomore year we were loaded. Overloaded, really. Hugh Green and Ricky Jackson, both future Pro Bowlers, were linebackers. The starting defensive linemen and cornerbacks had pro careers. The offensive line had three—Jimbo Covert, Mark May, Bill Fralic—and Russ Grimm, who only played 11 years on those great Washington teams. We had such talent that year that future NFL stars like Chris Doleman and Bill Maas couldn't crack the lineup.

And we didn't win a national title. Didn't get a chance at it, actually. Even though we were ranked second, the Sugar Bowl took Notre Dame to play top-ranked Georgia. So don't get me started about the bowl system.

"We'll play Georgia at 1 p.m., Notre Dame at 4 p.m., and then we'll see who the

19

champion is," I'd say to people that year.

(I enjoyed that line so much that later, with the Dolphins, I'd change it to needle certain coaches or teammates when they'd brag about University of Miami and Florida State teams. "My 1980 Pitt team could beat Miami at 1 p.m., and Florida State at 4 p.m., and . . .")

To this day, we were the best college team I've seen. Not that I'm biased or anything. But we finished with another ho-hum 11–1 season that year, just like each of my first three years at Pitt. Everything was blue skies for me. Sherrill opened up the offense my junior year. I led the country then with 37 touchdown passes. The Los Angeles Express were impressed enough to make me the United States Football League's top draft pick, and it

was such a surprise I didn't know where to turn for help. Matt Cavanaugh, who preceded me as Pitt's quarterback, introduced me to his agent, Nick Buoniconti. So I flew to Miami for the first time in my life to meet Nick. We even watched a Dolphins game together in the Orange Bowl.

Someone might have predicted I'd play there soon.

No one could have predicted the twisted path I'd take, though.

First of all, the Express didn't come up with the $40 million that a new owner did the following year for Steve Young. If they had, it might have been a tougher decision. They offered me something like $800,000, which was big money. Huge money for my family. But as a top NFL pick I'd make more, in an established league, on the kind of stage I'd been dreaming of all my life. Plus, I was a few credits short of my degree, so I figured to complete that circle.

And then the bottom fell out my senior year. Nothing went right. It was the first time I struggled, the first time people doubted my game, and the only time other than my final Dolphins season that I threw more interceptions than touchdowns.

But I've tried, at every step in life, to find a lesson. And accepting criticism with the same grace that you do the applause is something every young athlete needs to learn. It's never fun to play poorly or to be questioned. It certainly wasn't for me that senior

year at Pitt. But I think it served me well to learn how to handle everything that came with the game's ups and downs. Some people call it growing another layer of skin. I just call it growing up.

That senior season led to another one of life's great mysteries, right up there with the Lochness Monster and the Bermuda Triangle. The 1983 NFL draft. What happened? Why did my stock fall? How come I was the last of six quarterbacks taken (not to mention the third Pitt player)? To this day, I just shrug my shoulders, roll my eyes, and end up saying, "Thank you." Strange how the lowest moments turn into

the biggest blessings.

Of course, I wasn't thanking anyone as my name went uncalled for so long that draft day. I was home with some friends and family wondering what was happening. Some scouts had said I'd be gone in the top five picks. Well, those came and went and the only quarterback taken was Elway by the Colts, even though he'd told them not to bother.

Kansas City was picking seventh. I thought this was it. Their coach, John Mackovic, came to Pittsburgh two days before the draft to look at me.

"Listen, I'm picking a quarterback," he told me. "I'm working you out, then going to work out Todd Blackledge. I'm going to take one of you."

He took Blackledge.

Detroit had talked with me a lot, but they took Florida running back James Jones with the 13th pick. Buffalo took Jim Kelly next at number 14. New England took Tony Eason at number 15. And now the big slide through the day was fully under way. Frustrated? Confused? Who wouldn't be?

At one point, as we watched in disappointment, my father turned to me with words I took to heart. "Look," he said, "no matter what happens, you know you can play, and you know you're as good as any of these guys picked ahead of you. You'll have your opportunity to prove it."

Pittsburgh, picking 21st and needing a quarterback, chose defensive tackle Gabe Rivera. That hurt. Of course, whenever Steelers owner Art Rooney would see me in the coming years, he'd make a point to come up and say something about how wrong they were.

The Jets had the 24th pick. They had talked to me the day before the draft and suggested they'd take me if I would be there. Didn't come out and say it. But suggested it. Instead, they took Ken O'Brien. When his name was announced, Dolphins coach Don Shula turned to his scouts and said, completely seriously, "Who's he?"

And then he celebrated.

So that's how I became a Dolphin. They had never called me, never worked me out, never talked to me after the Indianapolis combine. Shula loved me from the combine, I learned later.

"Do we have a chance to get him?" he'd ask his personnel people.

"None at all," he had been told.

And yet there my phone finally was ringing three minutes before the end of the Dolphins pick. And there was Chuck Connor, their personnel director, saying coach Shula wanted to talk to me.

"Hey, you want to come to Miami? Because we need a quarterback," Shula said.

"You bet," I said.

It was as simple as that. Strange as that, too. But my disappointing senior season, the unsettling draft, the critics, the questions, all of it served one purpose. It assured I would be in the best shape possible for my first training camp. I worked my butt off that summer in hope of making a good first impression.

I couldn't have walked into a better situation as a rookie, either. The Dolphins had just gone to the Super Bowl. They had a tough, talented offensive line centered by Dwight Stephenson, a Hall of Famer. They had veteran playmakers like Tony Nathan and Nat Moore, as well as young talent like Mark Duper and Mark Clayton. They had a great defense called the Killer B's, taken from many of their last names: Betters, Baumhower, Bokamper, Brudzinski, Bowser, and the Blackwood brothers, Glenn and Lyle.

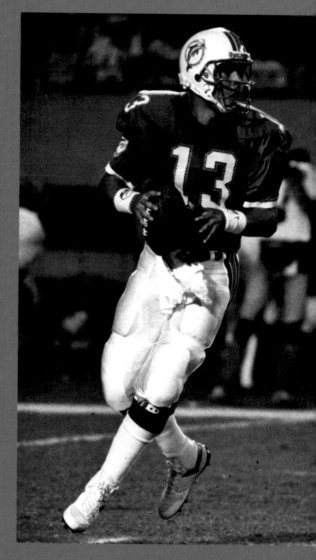

24

Little did I know then it was the best collection of talent I'd ever be around in the pros. I had great teammates throughout my career, guys who helped me every step and became great friends. But this group was strong at every position. All they needed was a quarterback, evidently. And, right from the start, Don Shula was the perfect coach to help develop me into one quickly.

"I want you to prepare like you have a chance to start the first time out," he told me. "Even in training camp, compete like you're starting."

He pushed me that way. He demanded I call my own plays in practices and exhibition games. That may sound like a small thing, but it enabled bigger, quicker strides.

You see, in most practices, an offensive coordinator will stand by the huddle and tell the quarterback the play. The quarterback then will repeat it in the huddle. So the quarterback doesn't have to think about the play so much as react to it. By calling my own plays, I had to study hard and be prepared for any situation unless I wanted to embarrass myself. If we were practicing first-and-10 passing situations, I'd need to know several plays before entering the huddle. Same for short-yardage, goal-line, or whatever other situation we were put in. Sometimes I'd screw up, and the coaches would correct me. But through it all my learning curve was shortened.

I also did something else right at the start that would accelerate my NFL education. I went up to Don Strock, introduced myself, and said, "Hey, I'm look-ing forward to you."

Strock later said that impressed him, the rookie approaching his competition like that. Strock and David Woodley had just taken the Dolphins to the Super Bowl in 1982, trading off at quarterback in what the media called "Woodstrock." But I wasn't just trying to be a good teammate by reaching out to Strock. I wanted to learn as much from him as possible. And, as it worked, I also got something more out of the deal. I got a lifelong friend.

That camp, too, I noticed something else. There was this brash rookie receiver from Louisville with whom I felt an immediate on-field bond. With Duper, it would develop later. But right from the first practices, maybe because as rookies we practiced together more, Mark Clayton and I made that intangible and indescribable connection that great passing combinations have. He knew what I sensed. I saw what he did. We also had similarly fiery on-field personalities, as everyone saw through the years, though I had a closing comeback for him right away.

You see, my Pitt team had beaten his Louisville team the year before, 63–0. And I never let him forget it.

"Hey, I had 10 catches that game," he'd say.

"I don't even remember you being there," I'd answer.

We joked that way, most everyone on that team. Strock. Clayton. Duper. Joe Rose. Bruce Hardy. But when it came to football, it was all about winning. My first start came in the sixth game of the year against Buffalo. We were 3–2. We fell behind at the start of the game, 14–0, But in the second half I completed 14 of 20 passes for 268 yards and three touchdowns to put us ahead 35–28 with three minutes left. We lost in overtime. But, for once, no one talked too much of a loss. Even Shula.

"The thrill is back," he told reporters after that game.

He saw the magic carpet going up. Everyone did. Nat Moore had become so tired of blocking and not catching passes in the previously button-downed offense that he entered 1983 figuring it would be his final season. It wasn't fun anymore. Then he saw how everything changed, how the ball started to be flung around like confetti, and he kept

26

playing a few more seasons. That tells how we all felt. Before I started against Buffalo, the offense had scored more than 14 points in just one of five games. From Buffalo on, we scored less than 20 points only once. I missed two games with a knee sprain, but we won 8 of the final 10 games, finishing 12–4. I led the league in passing. I was named Rookie of the Year and the first rookie quarterback to start a Pro Bowl.

And that only served as an introduction to 1984.

You have to understand something about that 1984 season: we didn't set out to break all the passing records. Break 'em? We didn't even know about them. When Peyton Manning broke my record of 48 touchdown passes by one touchdown in 2004, it was preceded for months with charts, updates, and weekly TV debates. Would he make it? Could he? What did he need to average over the final eight weeks? Then seven. Then six. . . .

It was nothing like that when I broke the existing record of 36 TD passes in 1984. I remember a Dolphins public-relations official stopping me one week.

"If you throw a few more TD passes today, you're going to break the record and people will want to talk about it," he said.

That's how I first paid any attention to it. We weren't trying to set a new standard.

27

We weren't realizing we were going to zoom by it with a month left to play. We were just trying to win games in the best way possible. And, OK, have some fun, too. We always had fun. "Pick a guy, and let it fly!" I'd say of my philosophy. Some team-mates came up with their own line: "If Dan ain't throwin', we ain't goin'!"

We put the ball in the air right from the first game (when I threw five touchdowns and no interceptions as we beat Super Bowl runner-up Washington) through the last games (four TD passes each of the final four regular-season games).

What I love about the record is that it came in the natural process of competing. The 36th touchdown pass to tight end Bruce Hardy cemented a 28–17 win on *Monday Night Football.* The 37th, to Mark Clayton, came early the following game in a loss at Oakland, one of just two that regular season. We kept scoring after that, and scoring, and scoring, all the way to the Super Bowl, where San Francisco sacked me four times, intercepted me twice, and swallowed up our dream season with one of their own. Hey, sometimes you lose. That's how I took it.

"We'll be back next year," I thought.

Talk about your mistakes of youth.

But how was I to know this would be my only chance? How was anyone? A lot of people have given reasons why I never got a Super Bowl ring. Didn't have a great running back. Didn't have a great defense. And, when there finally was a defense at the end after Jimmy Johnson took over, the offense needed some rebuilding.

Me, I just tell the story of Tommy Flynn. He was the quarterback whose Penn Hills High team went to the Pennsylvania championship when I was the state's big name. We became college roommates at Pitt. He was a fifth-round pick of Green Bay, played for a couple of years as a defensive back, and then was cut midway through the 1986 season. The New York Giants picked him up for the final two games that season. Then he blocked a punt in the playoffs. Then he was in the Super Bowl. And today he has a Super Bowl ring from that year. I'm happy for Tommy. I really am. He's a good friend. But if you're asking whether I'd trade my career for his ring . . .

That's not to say I haven't missed out on something. When John Elway won his first Super Bowl in 1998 after chasing it for as long as I had, my eyes misted up when he held that trophy over his head. I was that happy for him, that touched by the scene. I was jealous, too. I'll regret not knowing what he felt like that day, walking off

that last football field of the season a winner. I've come off it every other way: elated, dejected, even injured; on grass, turf, and dirt; in overtime and prime time; on Sunday, Monday, or Thursday; in any kind of regular-season and every kind of post-season game.

Every feeling you can imagine.

Except that one.

Maybe it's to keep me humble. Maybe I've got so many blessings, in so many areas, this is just something where God says, "Trust me, it's for your own good."

I've never felt defined by not getting a ring. Just like I've never felt the record books tell my full story. I'm proud of them all. Most touchdowns. Most passing yards. Most completions. You can go down the full list. But there's one number that's not in the record books—and never officially will be—that I might be most proud about: starting 145 consecutive games.

That's by my count, at least. You never read it that way, because the two scab games played during the 1987 players' strike officially interrupted the streak according to the NFL gatekeepers. I sure didn't play in those. I used to kid Ron Jaworski that he didn't have the streak, even though he had the record at 116 consecutive starts until the incredible Brett Favre started more than 200 games (and he's still playing).

Still, the way most people figure it, I started every Dolphins game for more than a decade beginning after the knee sprain of my rookie season. I had my right knee operated on five times during the streak. But I never missed a game. I broke a rib and hurt an elbow and a shoulder all within a few weeks in 1989. Didn't practice for a month.

But I played every game.

In 1992, I was clobbered by two Seattle players

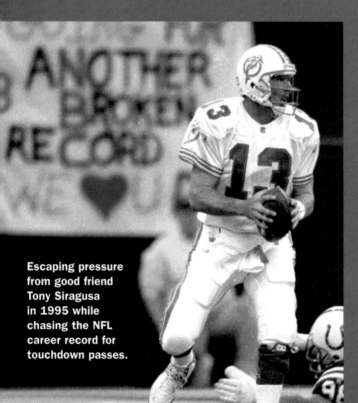

Escaping pressure from good friend Tony Siragusa in 1995 while chasing the NFL career record for touchdown passes.

30

and suffered a concussion. I only had two concussions in my career, and this was the worse one. I missed one play, took some smelling salts, jogged back on the field, and threw the winning touchdown pass in a 19–17 victory. Five minutes later, I couldn't remember what I'd done.

But I was ready the next game.

There were a lot of tough guys on those Dolphins teams, and I'd like to think I was one of them. You can't play injured, but you had to play hurt. I did that. The streak said you were there week after week for your teammates, your coaches, your fans. They could count on you. That's important in a team game. So there I was, every Sunday for more than a decade, until one sunny afternoon in Cleveland in 1993, when I dropped back on an ordinary play, went to throw an ordinary pass, and—pop!—nothing felt ordinary at all. My Achilles tendon snapped. It felt like I'd been shot. And the pain only got worse as I sat on the sideline the rest of that year, watching the games go on, missing out on all the fun, waiting for the next season and wondering when I'd be back. *If* I'd be back.

Whether you're a doctor, a salesman, a teacher, it doesn't matter. Everyone gets slapped in the face by something across a long career. A change. A move. A loss. Something. And most people come to the same conclusion I did at that point: man, look what you've taken for granted. Not wasted. Not grown tired of doing. But after 145 straight starts, after a decade of touchdowns and victories, I'd taken for granted that

It took a snapped Achilles tendon in a 1993 game against Cleveland to break a string of more than a decade's worth of consecutive starts.

31

Sundays would always be there for me. And now they weren't. And, boy, did I miss them.

After surgery, the tendon still wasn't right. It was too long, and I couldn't rise up on my toes. That meant the calf couldn't be strengthened. It also meant certain adjustments had to be made in my throwing. But no 10-year veteran looked forward to a training camp more than I did that summer, and none worked harder to try to retrieve my football world. Could I? Would I?

Questions like that swirl in your mind at those times, and that's why the 1994 opener against New England meant so much. I've had my share of wins. A few stand out. Like beating the Chicago Bears in 1985, when we spread out their famed "46 Defense" and assured the Dolphins franchise would keep the only Perfect Season. That was big. Or winning in the Meadowlands on the "Clock Play" against the Jets, pretending to spike the ball to stop the clock and instead throwing for the winning touchdown to Mark Ingram. That was big, too.

But no game was bigger for me personally than the 1994 opener against New England. Drew Bledsoe threw four touchdowns for the Patriots that day. I threw five.

And we needed them all. The fifth was the trickiest and most important. Fourth down. Ball at the Patriots' 39. Three minutes to go. We trailed by three points, and needed 5 yards for a first down. The called play was a short pass for a first down. But coming to the line I noticed Irving Fryar had the kind of one-on-one, bump-and-

run coverage that through the years I always took a shot on. Duper. Clayton. Fryar. Just make some eye contact to set the play at the line and go long.

But would I do it this first game back, with the day on the line?

Was there any doubt?

After the touchdown, after we celebrated, after the 39–35 win, even Patriots coach Bill Parcells walked over, shook my hand, and said, "Not bad for a guy on one ankle."

The Achilles has never been the same. I still can't lift up my right heel. And there's a pin in the ankle now, thanks to it being broken in 1996. Still, one of the most painful hits I ever took was in Indianapolis from a defensive back named Damon Watts. No one else probably even remembers him. Watts caught me on a blitz and slammed me to the turf on my left hip. It burned most of the game. But I had torn cartilage in my left knee earlier that game and figured that was the big problem. I even went to bed that night planning for knee surgery the next day.

I woke up in the middle of the night, sweating. My hip looked like a watermelon was stuffed inside it. My wife Claire called the hospital. I passed out on the way there. There was internal bleeding, as it turns out, and they ended up keeping a tube in me. Blood was pushed out for the next two weeks. Nasty sight. Nasty stuff.

33

By then my career had outlasted the Orange Bowl, outlasted owner Joe Robbie, and outlasted even Shula. Jimmy Johnson replaced him in 1996. And as disappointing as it was to see Shula leave, I bought into Jimmy's ideas. Build through the draft. Develop young talent. Construct a powerhouse for years. Everything he did in Dallas he attempted to do with the Dolphins.

How it worked out depends on how you look at it. We didn't make the Super Bowl. We didn't construct a dynasty. But I've never been a negative guy, and so I see the good things. He built enough in a year to make the playoffs in 1997. We won a

34

Accompanied by (from left) Joe Rose, who caught the first Marino NFL touchdown pass, Blair Buswell, sculptor of the Hall of Fame bust, and Oronde Gadsden, who caught the final TD pass of a record-breaking career.

playoff game in 1998. We won another in 1999, in Seattle, with an 85-yard touch-down drive with less than two minutes to go.

There would have been better ways to go out than a 62–7 loss in Jacksonville. Heck, any way might have been better, including on a shield. That one sat like a stone in your stomach, but that's how it goes. Sports aren't a Shakespeare play or a Fellini film. You don't get to write your own script. You don't get to set up your own scenes. You just take the games as they come, and for most of 17 seasons they came better than I could have expected.

What do I miss?

What *don't* I?

The guys. The games. The tingly feeling of strutting into an opponent's stadium, on a big day, with all their fans screaming—like you're on a mission. It's a feeling you can't duplicate or fully explain.

You know what? I even miss the practices. That may sound strange, but I miss standing out there, working on a play, getting the timing down with a receiver, throwing the ball over and over as the summer sun hovers, your body leaking buckets of sweat and your arm smoking from all the work. You get the play down well, then better. And then even better. And still you keep at it. That's what it's all about, you know? Teammates and teamwork and sweating together toward the next step, what-ever that step is, wherever it takes you.

It's taken me, ultimately, to Canton.

That's a long way from Parkview Avenue.

But it's been fun, the way I went, throwing a football the whole way there.

36

the early years

Here's something that surprises some people about my Central Catholic High School career:

I was also the kicker.

I loved it, too. One game I threw three touchdowns, and kicked an extra point, and we won, 19–18. The more things you can do, the more ways you can help the team win, the way I figured it.

Everyone knew where I could help most, though. I threw on 39 of 55 offensive plays in one game. So on kickoffs, after kicking the ball down-field, I'd be smart enough to follow the coaching instructions and run near the referee so I wouldn't get hurt by some kamikaze block.

Central Catholic had the best football program in Pittsburgh at that time—still does, for that matter, as it won the Pennsylvania state title in 2004.

And I set out early on to attend there, even going to summer school after eighth grade to have the necessary grades. The school was just a short trip there from my home, and an even shorter one up Fifth Avenue to my next stop: the University of Pittsburgh.

Those were some years at Pitt. My first collegiate pass was an interception against Kansas. I didn't get rattled. My third pass was a touchdown. I guess my teammates were struck by that kind of composure, because Hugh Green soon hung a nickname on me that followed me through Pitt: "Ice."

37

That's what I'm still called, The guys still call me that when we get together and replay the good times. There were plenty of them, too, as we went 33–3 my first three years.

To tell you the talent we had on those teams, my sophomore year, all 22 starters were drafted in the NFL. My junior year, I led the country with 37 touchdown passes, and the final one is a favorite memory of mine.

Sugar Bowl, 1981.

Forty-two seconds left.

Fourth-and-5 at the Georgia 33. We're down three points. And they blitzed. They tried to win the game, right there, and we turned it around on them. Our backs picked up the blitz, I found tight end John Brown for the winning touchdown, and it was so dramatic you can still watch it today on ESPN Classic.

My kids get a kick out of watching it.

I tell them it was a bigger kick to do it.

39

The talent at Pitt was unbelievable in
those days, including offensive linemen
(page 38, center photo, from left) Jim
Sweeney, Jimbo Covert, Moose Sams,
Emil Boures, Terry Quirin, Bill Fralic,
Paul Dunn, and Rob Fada.

Helping out the punting unit during a high school game at Central Catholic.

44

46

With high school sweetheart and future wife Claire after Super Bowl XIX at Stanford Stadium in 1985.

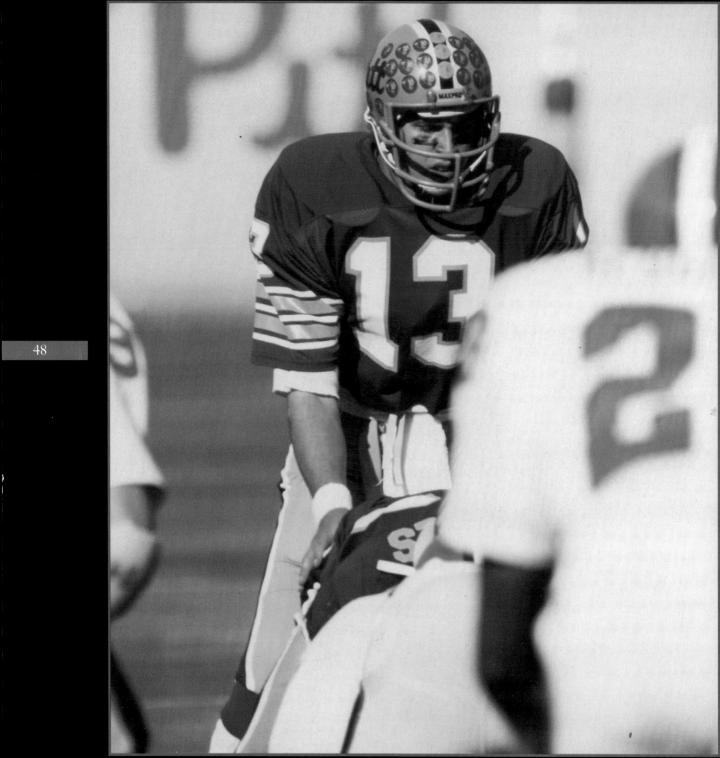

49

"Those were some years at Pitt. My first collegiate pass was an interception against Kansas. I didn't get rattled. My third pass was a touchdown."

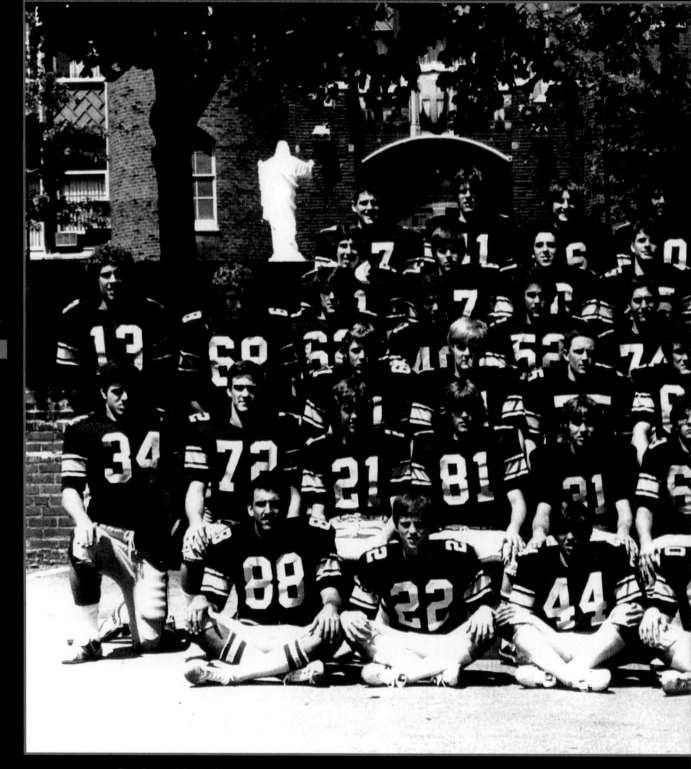

The Central Catholic squad in all its glory, featuring No. 13 in the third row, far left.

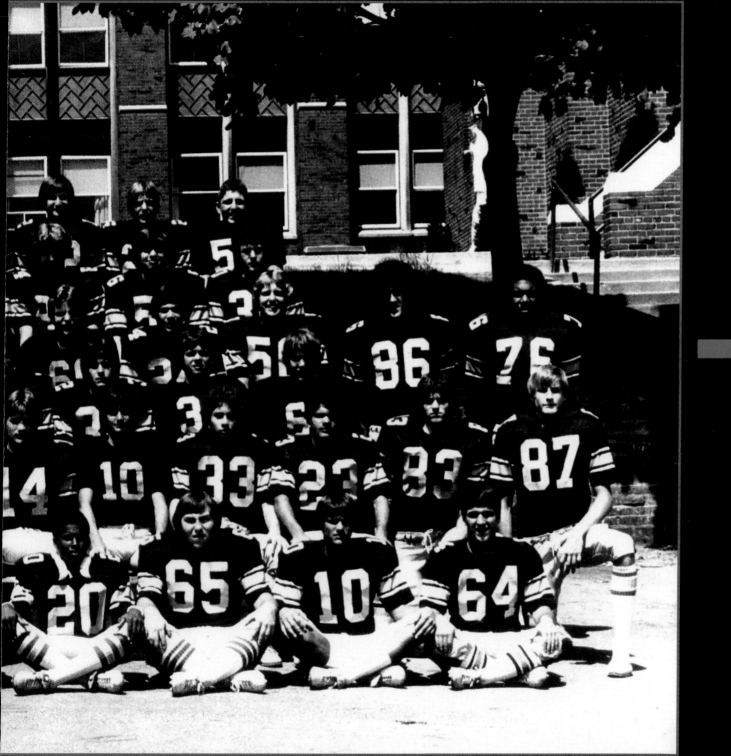

53

56

family life

Claire and I met back in high school, back when I was the quarterback at Central Catholic, though she insists she didn't know that at first.

I nod and say I believe her.

When people talk about not winning a Super Bowl ring, I understand why. It would be a nice accomplishment. But the most important ring in my life is the one I slipped on Claire's finger at St. Regis Catholic Church in Pittsburgh a couple of weeks after playing the Super Bowl in 1985.

We have six great kids, and I've learned something from each of them. One thing I've learned is how important it is that they follow their own passion. Take Daniel. He's the oldest, a high-school senior. From the time he was little, Daniel was a performer. He'd get up on a table and sing to the television. By age 8, he was doing plays at the Fort Lauderdale Children's Theatre. He's kept at it, too, getting bigger roles in school plays and working harder to get better while playing everything from England's King Henry II to the biblical Cain to the hot-dog-munching son of Dennis Quaid in a pool-side cameo in the movie *Any Given Sunday*.

Then there's Michael. He's two years younger than Daniel and plays football. I made it a point not to push any of my kids into football, though since he likes it I help him, just as my dad helped me. Michael also likes to play music. Especially rap music. And so in some respects I've discovered what my parents must have gone through at times with me. You need patience. Understanding. And, occasionally, ear plugs.

Joey is 15, and likes golf. As a freshman last year, his four-man high-school team finished fourth in the state. He hits the ball as long as I do. He says he can beat me, too, although I tell him I haven't seen it happen yet. Still, we make quite a team together.

We played in a father-son tournament in Ireland and finished third of 87 teams.

Then there's Alexandra. Ali, we call her. She was the first girl, so as any parent knows that was a nice change for us. She was into horseback riding for years, but she recently broke her thumb doing it and that cooled her on it a bit, for now. We'll see. Basketball. Volleyball. She's trying it all, just like any 13-year-old should.

As our first four children started to grow up, Claire and I decided we wanted a bigger family and came to an even bigger decision. We would adopt. And we ended up doing so in a way that broadened our perspective and enriched our lives. In 1998, Claire flew to China for two weeks and returned with Niki Lin, who was 2 years old at the time. Niki

is 9 now, and she has her own fun personality. On the basketball court, for instance, she puts up her hands and calls for the ball. But when it comes she backs away, suddenly not wanting it. In 2002, after working the Super Bowl for CBS, I came home to our sixth child: Lia had returned with Claire from China. She was 6 then, and the great thing is she immediately fit right into the family. Playing. Talking. Sharing. She also has a quality unique to her—she saves money. She'll come up to me with some money she's saved and tell me to put it in her account. Hey, what family couldn't use a smart money manager?

So that's our six children. No, they're not quite enough for a full offense, but sometimes, when everyone's on the move, we sure look like one.

A playful moment at the Marino home, with sons Michael, Daniel, and Joey.

60

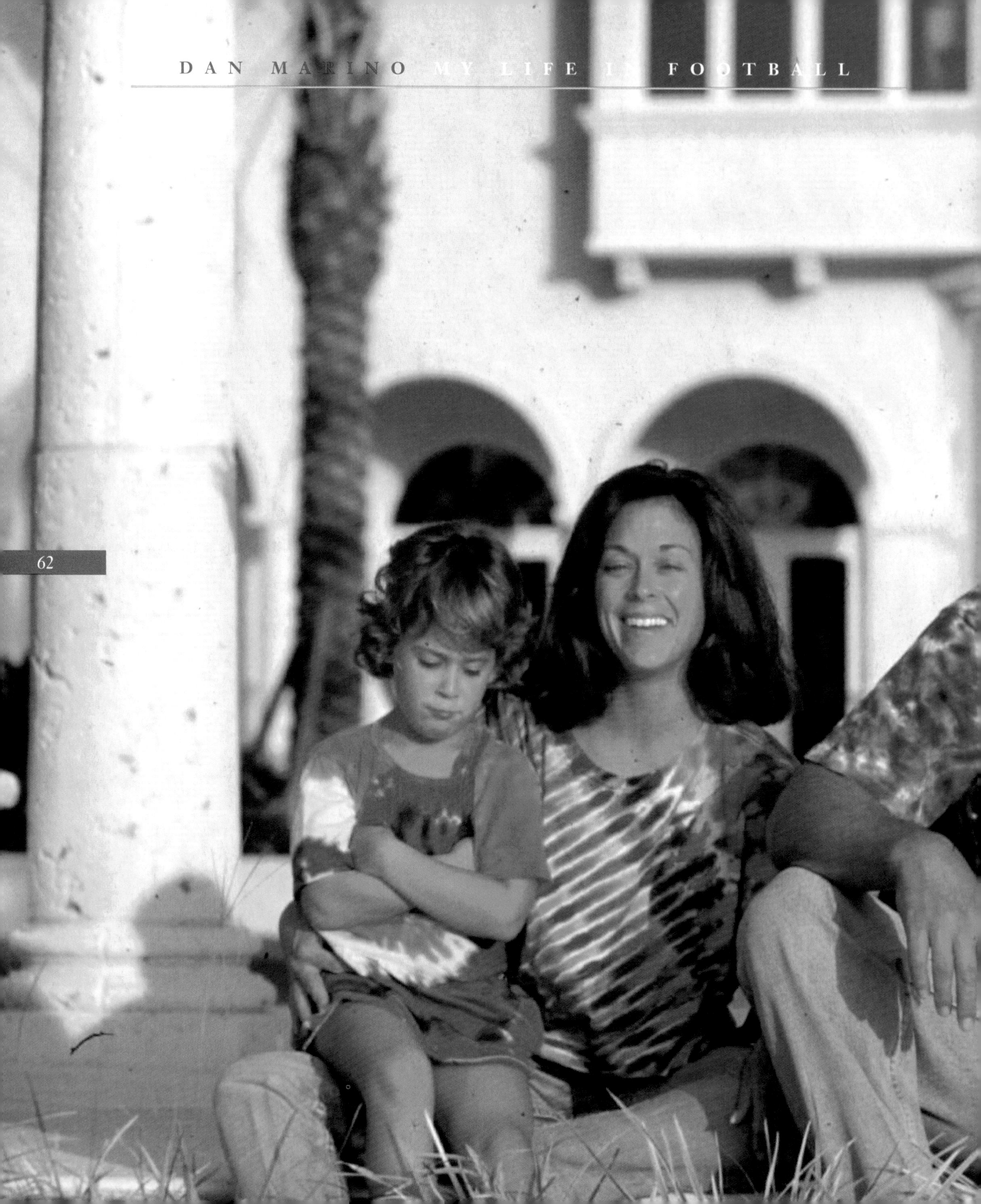

The whole family, with Daniel in the back row, Claire, Ali, Michael, and Joey in the middle, and Niki and Lia in front.

65

Sharing one of countless special moments over the years with Dan Sr.

With Claire at a charity event sponsored by Levinson's Jewelers.

70

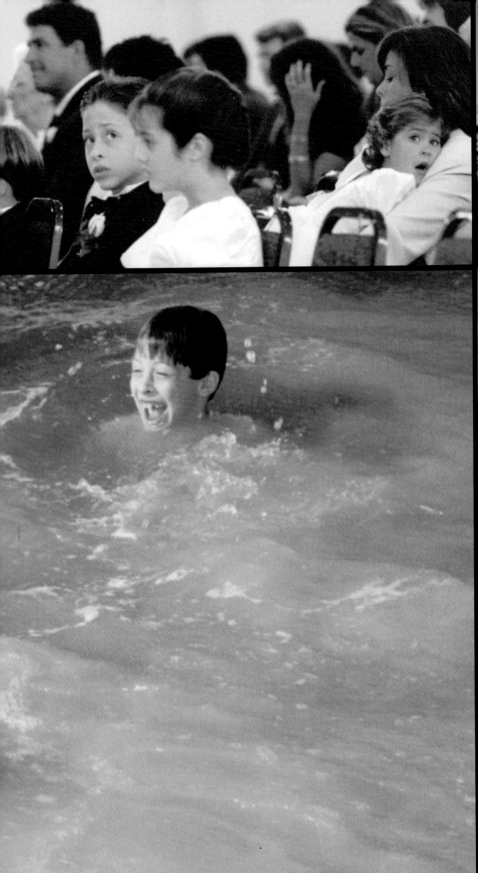

"We have six great kids, and I've learned something from each of them. One thing I've learned is how important it is that they follow their own passion."

Daughter Alexandra is an accomplished equestrian.

At the Miami Heat playoff game in May 2005 with Joey, Ali, and Michael.

The 2004 family Christmas portrait.

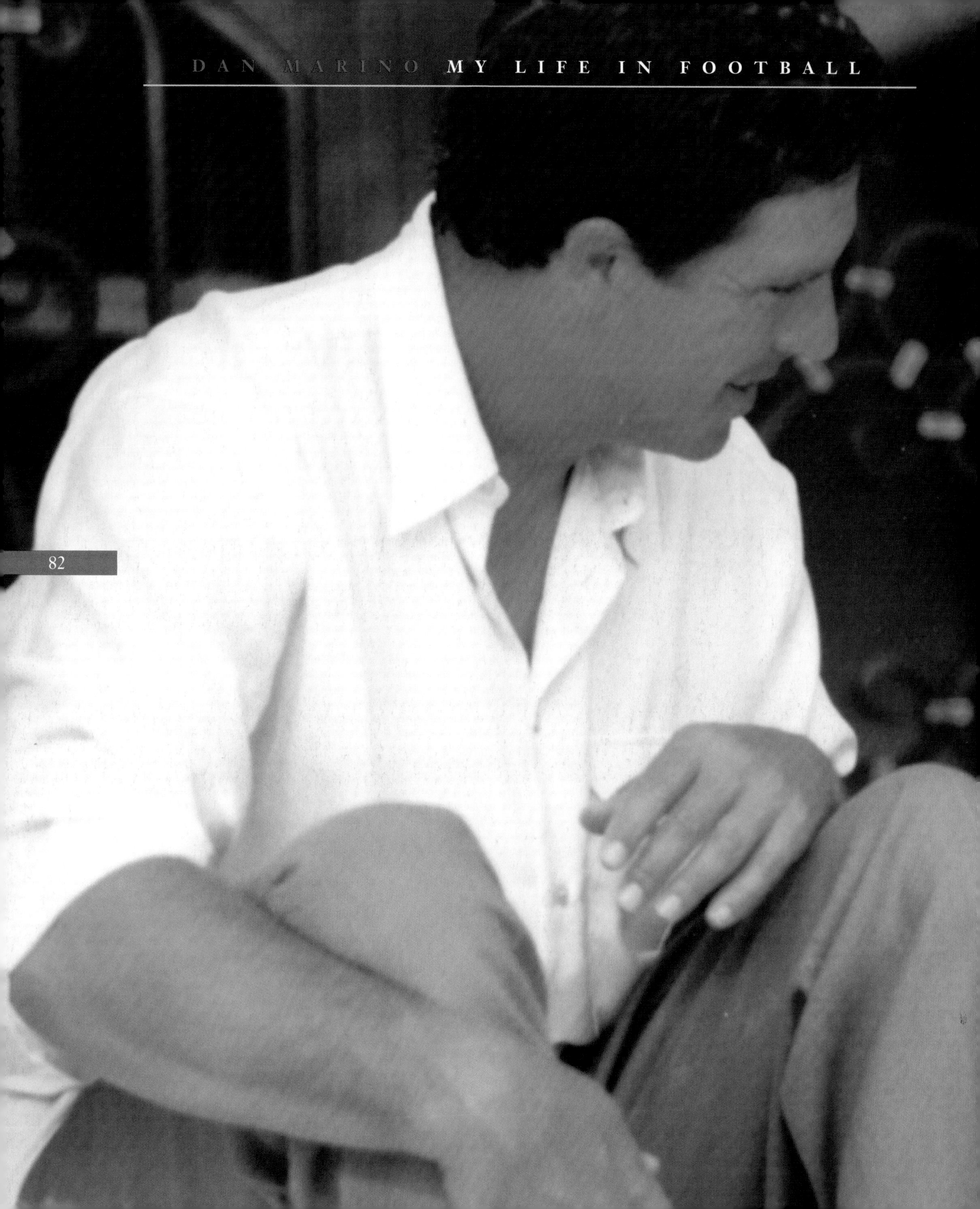

86

"Claire and I met
back in high school,
back when I was the
quarterback at Central
Catholic, though she
insists she didn't know
that at first. I nod and
say I believe her."

88

Out on the town with Mom, Dad, and sister
Debbie in the back row, and flanked by cousin
Dorothy Foster and grandmother Julia Marino.

92

a hall of
fame career

On my first play as a Dolphin in 1983, I ran confidently onto the field, stepped like a leader into the huddle, looked into the eyes of my team-mates, and showed all the composure any rookie would attempt.

And then I messed up calling the play. In fact, I did such a mangled job that veteran receiver Nat Moore stepped in and called it the right way.

"OK, it's on 'two,'" I said when he had finished. "Let's go."

You might say things improved a little from there for the next 17 seasons. I ended with 25 NFL records and tied for five others, though don't ask me to name them all. Some stand out. Most completions. Most yards passing. And most touchdowns, a mark that began that first day in Oakland. I threw my first touchdown pass, a 6-yarder to tight end Joe Rose, who had the presence of mind to keep the football.

Twelve seasons later, it was another 6-yard touchdown pass, this one to Keith Byars against Indianapolis, that was my 343rd touchdown to break the NFL mark. Touchdowns weren't just some stat to keep count of, though. They helped your team win. That's really why I take pride in throwing 420 of them across my years.

How much did I like touchdowns? Well, I named my dog Touchdown, prov-ing it was this man's best friend.

You don't succeed like I have in this sport without having great people help-ing you. The coaches. The line. The receivers, starting with Mark Duper and Mark Clayton, who were there my first 10 seasons and developed the kind of chemistry that comes with playing together. I have plenty of memories, like

94

the one game against the Jets, when I came to the line late in the game, and saw Duper lining up wide, one-on-one, with a corner-back. I looked at him and both our eyes widened. That's all we needed to do, besides run fast and throw long.

Touchdown.

We win, 21-17.

That's how it was on the best days.

Once in an ESPN interview with me and a cou-ple of other quarterbacks, a question came up about being in "the zone," where you feel nothing can go wrong on the field. The other guys described what that was like for them. Then it was my turn. And me?

"I feel like I've been in the zone for 10 years," I said.

Of course, that was asked after I'd been in the league 10 years.

Today, I might say it was like that for *17* years.

Former teammate and wide receiver extraordinaire Mark Duper was on hand to help celebrate the record-breaking 343rd career TD pass.

His win against the Colts was the 50th come-from-behind victory in a career that had its fair share of fantastic finishes.

"How much did I like touchdowns? Well, I named my dog Touchdown, proving it was this man's best friend... You don't succeed like I have in this sport without having great people helping you."

108

Leaving the field
for the last time,
following a devas-
tating playoff loss
in Jacksonville.

116

Sharing some laughs with the rest of the vaunted class of the 1983 draft, from left: John Elway, Todd Blackledge, Jim Kelly, Tony Eason, and Ken O'Brien.

"Touchdowns weren't just some stat to keep count of, though. They helped your team win. That's really why I take pride in throwing 420 of them across my years."

Win or lose, fulfilling your obligations to the media is as much a part of the game as anything else.

Catching up with John Elway after
a regular-season game in Miami.

127

129

An embrace with old friend and on-field rival Jim Kelly
following a regular-season game in Buffalo.

130

The Dolphins' prolific passing offense was the brain-child of offensive coordinator Gary Stevens (far right) and coach Shula (far left), with plenty of on-field help from some exceptional talent over the years.

A lighter moment in the locker room with friend and backup QB Bernie Kosar.

**Veteran quarterback Don Strock was an invaluable mentor from the first day
of training camp in 1983 and has turned out to be a lifelong friend.**

142

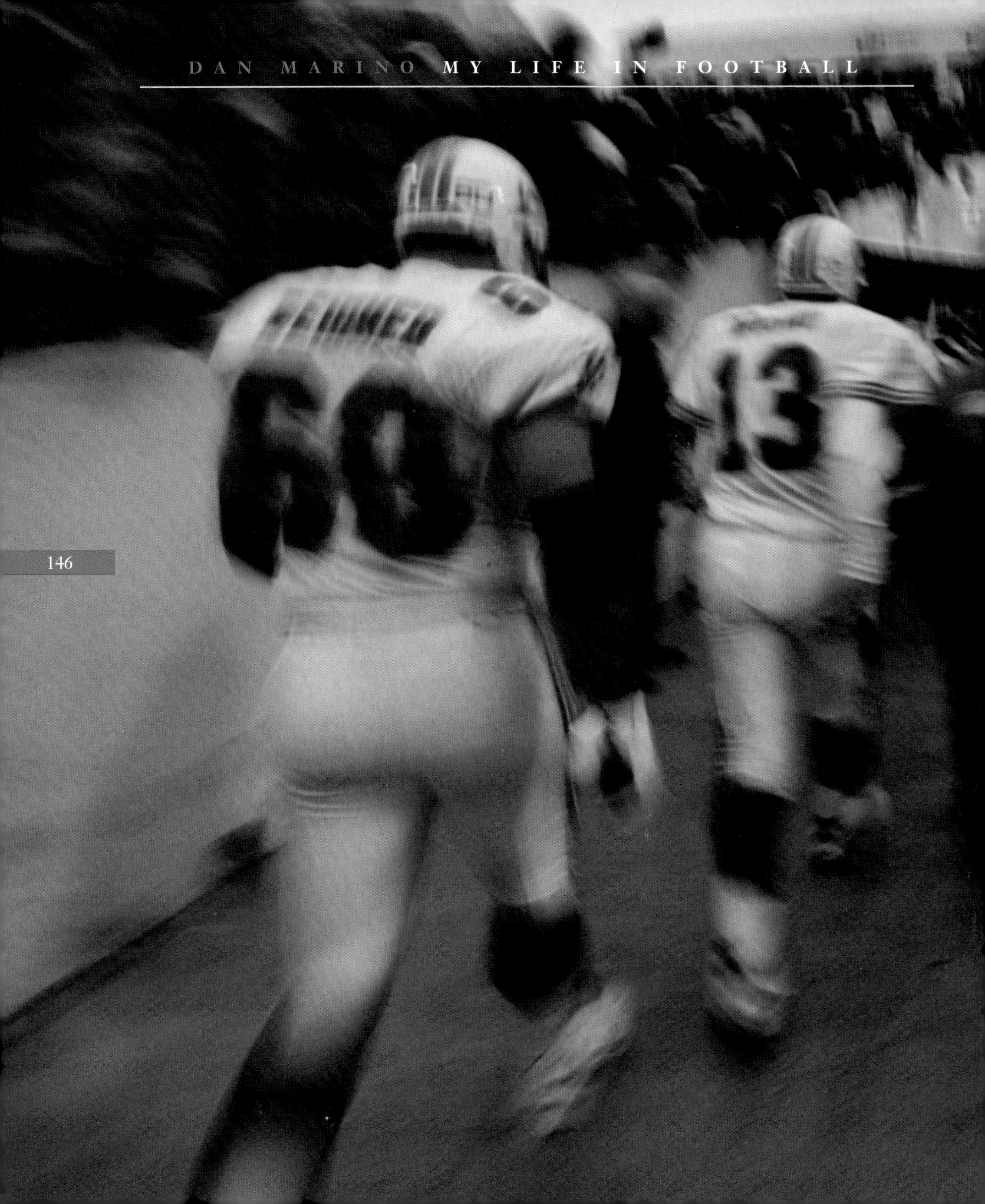

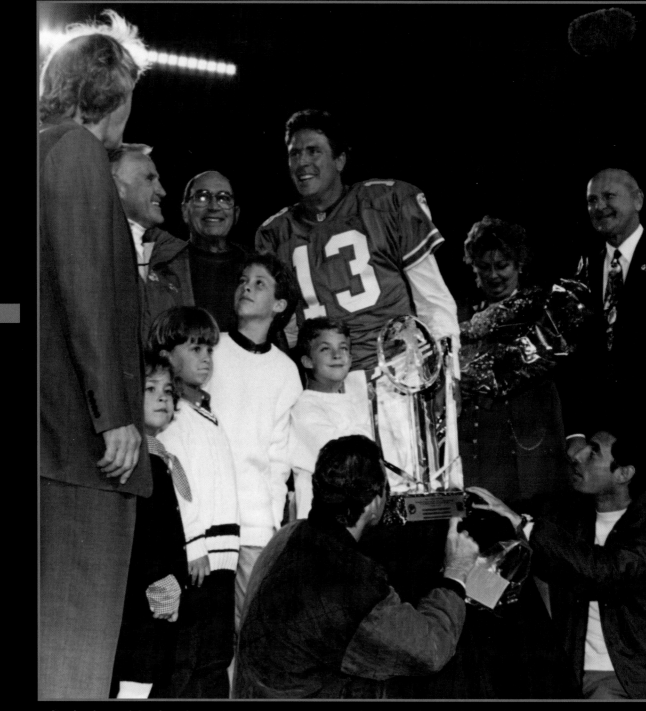

148

Sharing in a celebration of record-breaking proportions are family members, NFL legend Fran Tarkenton (far left), coach Shula (second from left), and Dolphins owner H. Wayne Huizenga.

150

living

the dream

Something strange happened on a recent golf trip in Ireland: the caddies treated me like a celebrity. But not because I was an NFL star. Not because I threw for a record number of touchdowns. Not because I won all those games and, played all those years, and not because they were big fans of the Dolphins.

The Dolphins?

The caddies hadn't even heard of them.

"You were in that Jim Carrey movie!" they shouted.

Yep, that was me being kidnapped by a transsexual kicker before the Super Bowl in the movie *Ace Ventura: Pet Detective*. OK, it didn't get me an Oscar. But it did get people advising me across the globe, because of a scene in the movie, "Hey, Dan, laces out!"

My football career has opened the door to a funhouse of perks like that movie. Things I never dreamed of. Things I never even *considered* dreaming of. Like being in the music video "Only Wanna Be With You" with Hootie and the Blowfish. Like starting the Daytona 500 or partnering a NASCAR race team. Like climbing 9,000 feet, straight up through the sky in an F-16 fighter jet, shouting as my chest zoomed out my spine, "This is incredible!"

I've had snowballs thrown at me on Isotoner glove commercials and opened my own line of mattresses. There are now five Dan Marino's Fine Food & Spirits (menu hint: try Dan's Tender Beef Tips). There was the time in 1988 when Dan Pohl and I won the AT&T Pebble Beach Pro-Am during the day, and I drank beers with Clint Eastwood at night.

I trade quips and insights on the set of CBS's studio show every Sunday from

152

New York (mentioning the "Clock Play," to former Jets quarterback Boomer Esiason wherever it fits, just for kicks). I'm on the set of HBO's show, *Inside the NFL*, for which I sometimes travel around doing features. Once, while doing a feature on the remake of the movie, *The Longest Yard*, they offered me a cameo (unfortunately, I was too busy).

Funny thing is, of all my movie memories, from being in Adam Sandler's *Little Nicky* to an upcoming cameo in Dave Barry's *Guy's Guide To Being A Guy*, one that stands out never came on the screen. This was on the set of Ace Ventura.

Everyone was running about, the director setting up scenes, the camera crew changing lenses, the grips moving equipment. A football sat there. I picked it up and tossed it to someone. He tossed it back. I tossed it to someone else.

Suddenly, people were taking off, running patterns, diving for balls.

Grips ran slants.

Lighting guys went deep.

Even the director, Tom Shadyac, ran a quick down-and-in and beat a Hollywood-style defensive back. "The catch of my life," he said.

Just another day in the dream.

At Daytona Speedway, not as ordinary racing fans but as part owners of a NASCAR team.

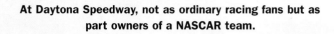

156

158

Excelling in professional sports led to some unbelievable opportunities, like the chance to fly with the Thunderbirds.

160

Capt Dan Torweihe
Narrator

TSgt Gordon Fenley
SrA Shawn Yoder

Carrying the Olympic torch in Miami with son Michael to help kick off the 2002 Winter Games in Salt Lake City.

On stage with Darius Rucker of Hootie and the Blowfish fame, and with pals John Elway and Jim Kelly (above).

"*My football career has opened the door to a funhouse of perks. Things I never dreamed of. Like being in the music video 'Only Wanna Be With You' with Hootie and the Blowfish. Like starting the Daytona 500 or partnering a NASCAR race team.*"

FEBRUARY 16 - 17, 1996
JOE ROBBIE STADIUM

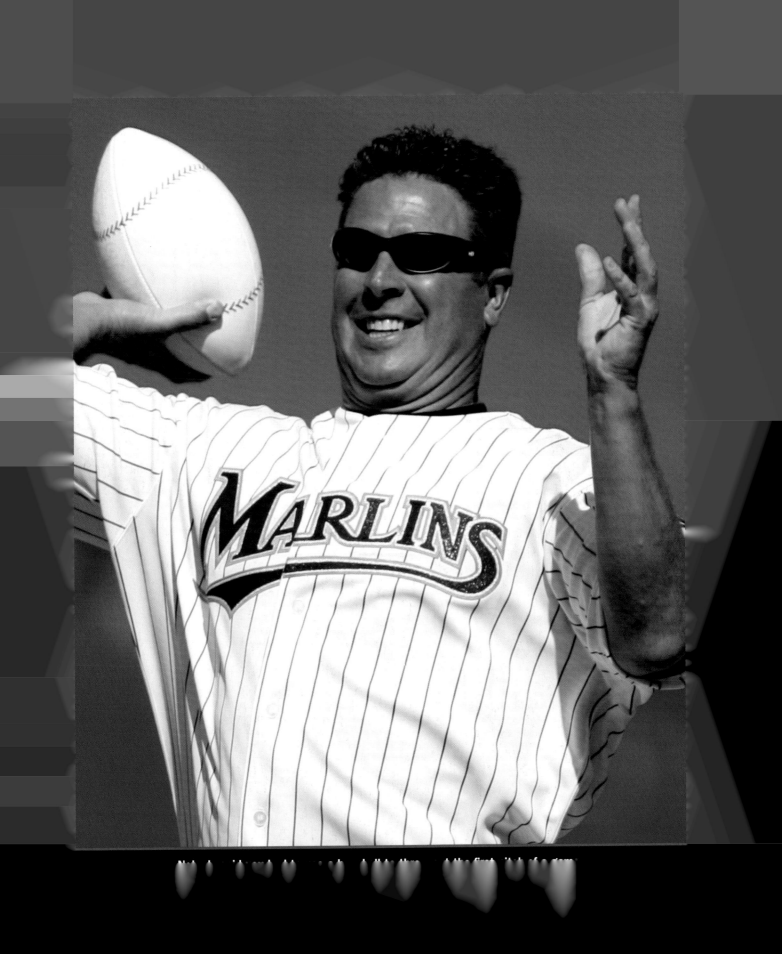

DAN MARINO BLVD

NW 199 ST — HONEY HILL DR

At a street-naming
ceremony in front of
Dolphins Stadium with
H. Wayne Huizenga.

giving back

Let's talk about what happens when you spend 17 years playing for one franchise. You make a difference with that team. You make a difference in the game, if you're lucky enough.

You also have a chance to make a difference in a community, if that's what you choose. You can grow with an area as you grow up. You can build relationships as you build your life. Sometimes you even find out your family's issues are like a lot of other families' issues, too, and that your standing in sports has a way of raising awareness to help everyone.

At least, that's what Claire and I found.

In 1991, we learned that our second son, Michael, had autism. It was a mild case, we discovered, as everything worked out and Michael began attending mainstream schools. But at the time, we were devastated. We felt helpless. We also were confused, going from coast to coast, specialist to specialist, to find the proper diagnosis and treatment.

One thing we weren't, we also found, was alone. A lot of people in our situation felt the same way we did. They just didn't have the financial means or standing as a professional athlete to help. Claire and I did, so we became national spokespersons for autism. The Dan Marino Foundation was started with the idea of helping needy children. In 2004, it gave more than $1.1 million to 30 agencies supporting autism research, medical treatments, and outreach programs at universities, hospitals, and special-needs organizations.

One of the places that gets foundation money is the Miami Children's Hospital Dan Marino Center in Weston. It provides what we saw Michael needed and

172

never found. It's a one-stop medical center, directed by Dr. Roberto Tuchman, where children with chronic medical problems, ranging from attention-deficit disorder to autism to brain tumors, can receive diagnosis and treatment.

Doctors, specialists, therapists—they're all here. So are kids and families from across the United States, South America, Europe, Asia, Africa. You name the place, chances are someone from there has visited. Many have moved to Miami just for the center. In 2004, it had more than 48,000 patient visits.

But the best part, the part that makes it all worthwhile, comes when strangers approach me with a story. Maybe their child had a problem. Maybe they were referred to the center. Maybe having all the help there in one place let their child get a quicker diagnosis, or better treatment, or the kind of help they hadn't previously found.

I just set out to throw a football.

It feels great making a difference.

174

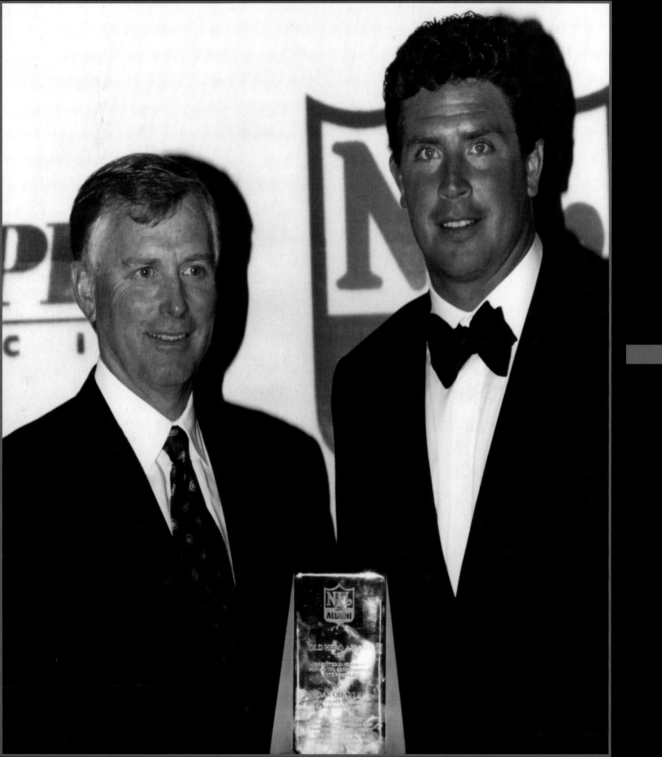

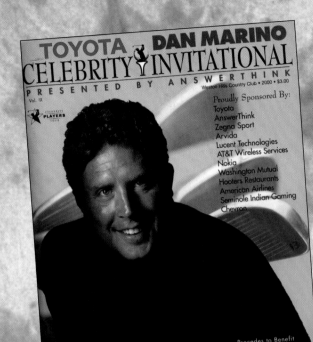

The Dan Marino Celebrity Invitational is an annual event that raises money for various children's charities in South Florida.

*memories
and
mementos*

I never collected football or baseball cards as a kid. Maybe I shouldn't say that considering the hundreds of cards I've appeared on. And maybe I shouldn't say how autographs and pictures didn't interest me much growing up, either. But they didn't. I remember a grade-school classmate got Hall of Fame linebacker Ray Nitschke to come to our football banquet. I met him. Shook his hand. Said hello. Felt the thrill of meeting a big-time athlete. And that was enough for me.

Still, I can understand why lots of people are interested in my memorabilia these days—and not just because I collect my stuff, too.

I can understand because there are certain things that I have made a point of finding or saving through the years that have meaning to me.

For instance, in the glass cabinet where I keep some of my milestone footballs I've also placed playing cards of other players: Terry Bradshaw, Willie Stargell, Roberto Clemente. Some of the legends of my Pittsburgh youth.

There's even a card of John Congemi, who followed me as the University of Pittsburgh's quarterback and has remained a good friend. He played nine years in the Canadian Football League.

"You've got to autograph me a card," I told him.

That's his card from the Toronto Argonauts beside Bradshaw, Stargell, and Clemente.

So you can say, in some respects, I've taken to collecting as an adult. The other stuff in that case at my home, and another case, and covering the walls of a couple of rooms at my home, you might expect to find. There are

helmets of the teams I played on. I even got one sent to me from St. Regis, my middle-school team, and I know it was my helmet because I recognized how a couple of the facemask bars were cut away by my dad so I could see.

There are the touchdown footballs at each century from 100 to 400. There are the footballs that mark each passing yardage landmark, starting at 30,000. There are pictures of me all along the way, like watching my career on time-elapse film.

There also are two other things that connect me with collectors. Two books. One is *The Science of Hitting* by Ted Williams. My dad gave a copy of it to me as a kid. I lost it somewhere along the way but bought a copy as a way of remembering, and connecting, which to me is what collecting is about.

The second book is *A Matter of Style* by Joe Namath. It meant something to me as a kid, reading it, hearing his thoughts.

184

Football Preview '94 • Conversation with Wayne

AUGUST/SEPTEMBER

SF
SPORTS
1994
THE SOUTH FLORIDA SPORTS MAGAZINE

HE'S BACK

MARINO

$2.50

FALL FASHION PREVIEW 3: The Best of Armani, Ferre, Versace & Valentino

GQ

SEPTEMBER $3.50

WHAT MEN WANT 2
OK, Let's Talk About Sex

EVERYBODY'S ALL-AMERICAN
Charles P. Pierce
On Peyton Manning

WALL STREET'S NEW FLIMFLAM ARTISTS
By Alan Deutschman

PLUS
Joe Queenan
Rants &
Alan Richman
Eats French

Dandy
Dan Marino
The Best Quarterback You'll Ever Se
By Peter Richmond

09>

OUR TOP 30
NBA DRAFT PICKS

NFL HOT TOPICS: Sex and drugs in Dallas

INSIDE
SPORTS

July 1996

The
Best QB Ever,
but... No Ring

National Football League
Record Book

Dolphins quarterback **Dan Marino** has set all the records—now he hopes Jimmy Johnson can make his Super Bowl dream come true

■ Baseball's hottest young sluggers
■ Athletes and HIV: Flirting with death

07>

BECKETT. TRIBUTE:

Dan Marino

U.S. $4.95 CAN $6.75 AUS $7.50
ISSUE 12

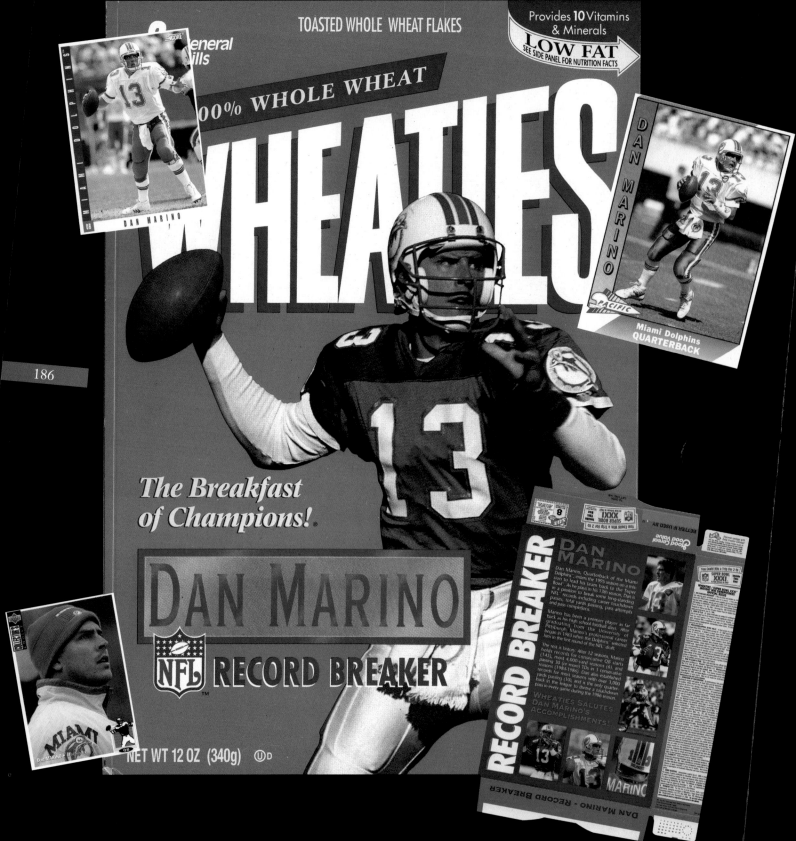

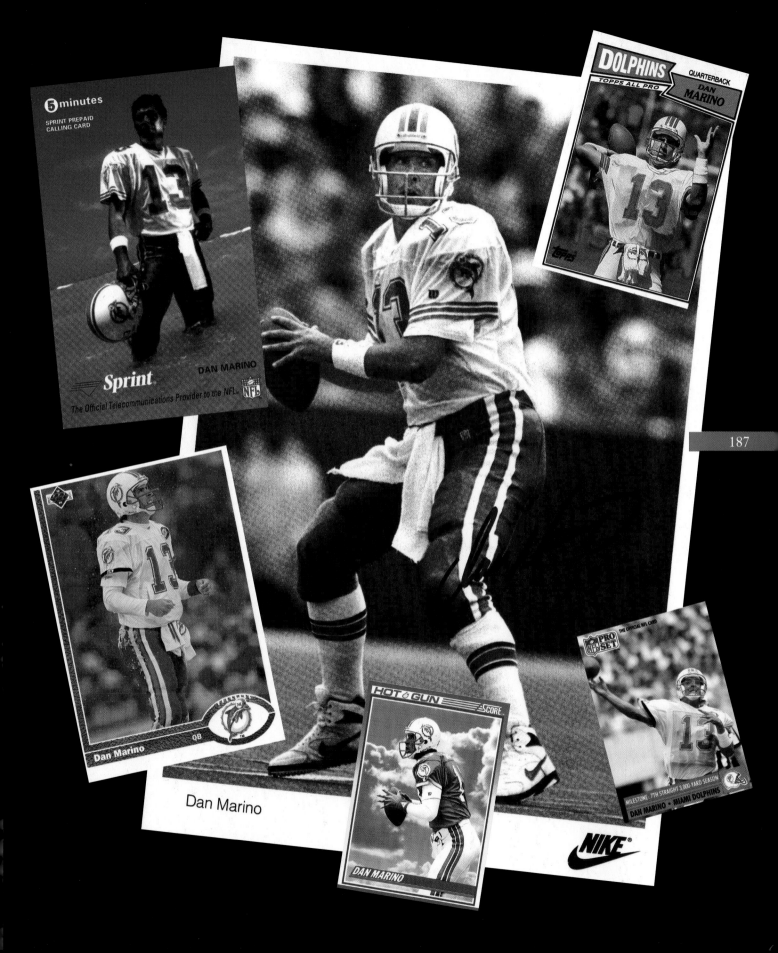

Dan Marino

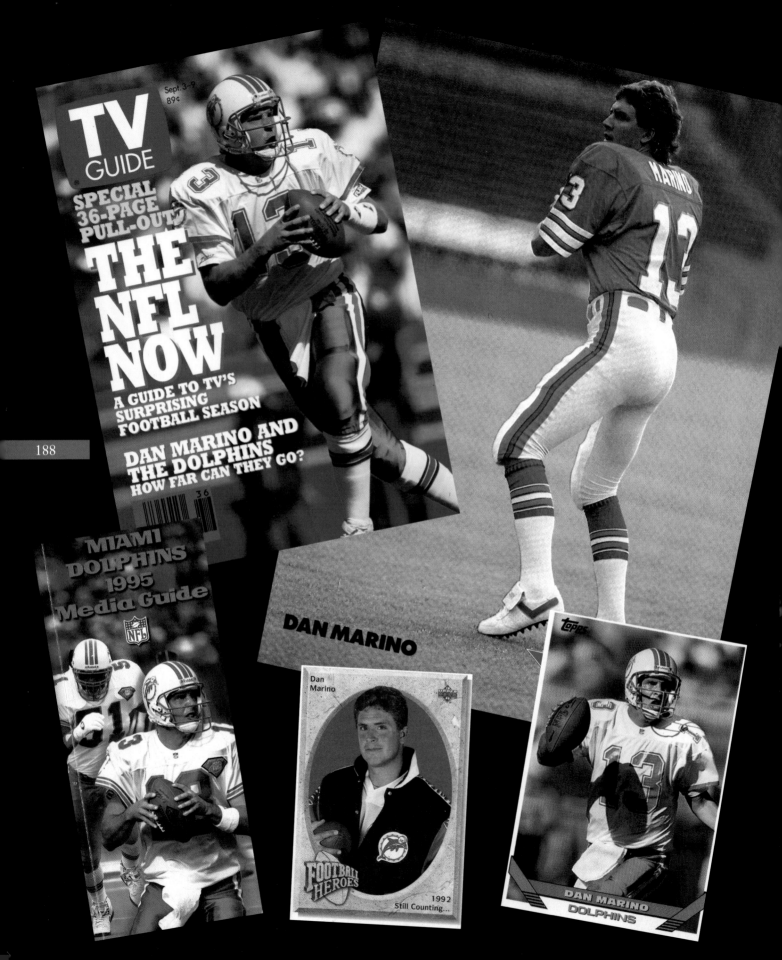

TV GUIDE

Sept. 3-9
89¢

SPECIAL
36-PAGE
PULL-OUT!

THE
NFL
NOW

A GUIDE TO TV'S
SURPRISING
FOOTBALL SEASON

DAN MARINO AND
THE DOLPHINS
HOW FAR CAN THEY GO?

36

MIAMI
DOLPHINS
1995
Media Guide

NFL

DAN MARINO

Dan
Marino

FOOTBALL
HEROES

1992
Still Counting...

Topps

DAN MARINO
DOLPHINS

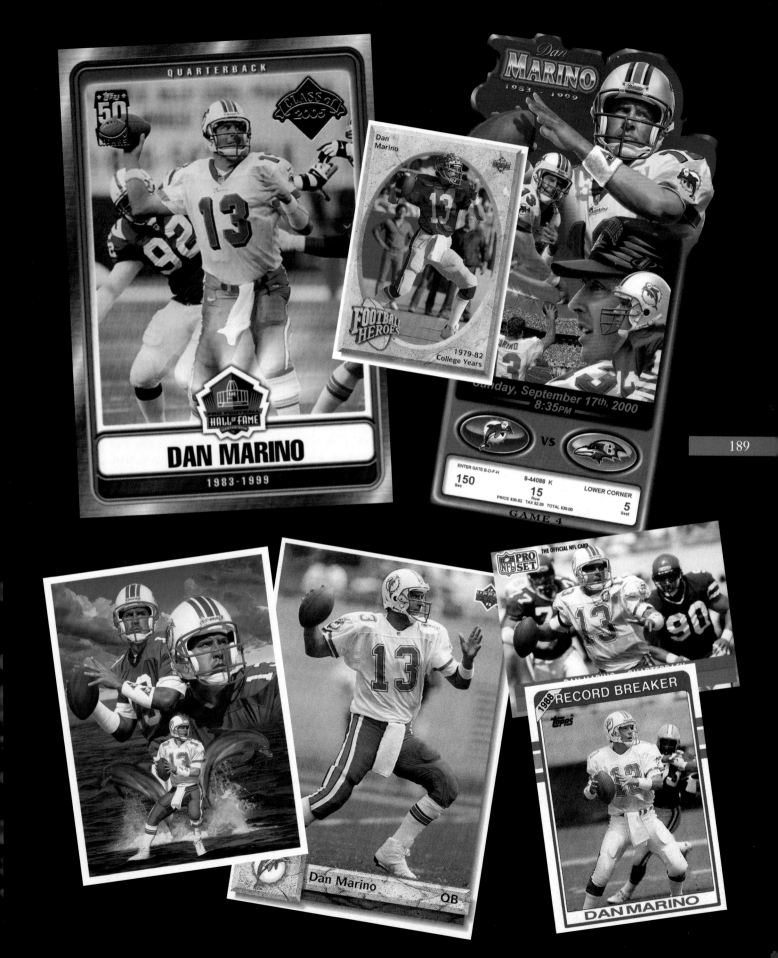

This book is available in quantity at special discounts for your group or organization.
For further information, contact:

Triumph Books
542 S. Dearborn St.
Suite 750
Chicago, Illinois 60605
(312) 939-3330
Fax: (312) 663-3557

Printed in the U.S.A.

ISBN-13: 978-1-57243-800-2

ISBN-10: 1-57243-800-2

Design by Robert A. Wyszkowski

Text by Dan Marino, with Dave Hyde

Photographs by Marc Serota, except where noted below:

Additional photo credits:

Courtesy of the Marino family: pages 15, 34, 172-173, 174-175
Courtesy of the Dan Marino Foundation: pages 178-179, 180
Courtesy of Central Catholic High School: pages 17, 18, 40-41, 42-43, 52-53
Courtesy of the University of Pittsburgh: pages 19, 20, 22, 38, 45, 48, 51 (right)
Courtesy of AP/Wide World Photos: pages 21, 23, 39, 44, 46-47, 49, 50, 52, 54-55, 141
Courtesy of Robert Duyos: page 138
Courtesy of Wireimages.com: page 153
Courtesy of Malcolm Farley: page 190